D1784159

THINKING SKILLS RESOURCE BOOK

LORENE • REID

Creative Learning Press, Inc.

P.O. Box 320, Mansfield Center, Connecticut 06250

COPYRIGHT © 1990 CREATIVE LEARNING PRESS, INC.
P.O. BOX 320, MANSFIELD CENTER, CT 06250
ALL RIGHTS RESERVED.

MANUFACTURED IN THE UNITED STATES OF AMERICA

ISBN 0-936386-58-4

TABLE OF CONTENTS

Page

INTRODUCTION

Every teacher should be a teacher of thinking, a professional who deliberately addresses thinking. The teacher is the key factor in a thinking classroom with control over the process, the skills, and attitudes. Key variables involved in effective thinking include

1. Content: Knowledge and information which forms the basis for thinking.

2. Skills: Process skills which teach students to think effectively.

3. Motivation: The environment which gives students a reason to think.

There are four components in a thinking classroom.

1. The teacher will create the climate where thinking is a valued activity.

2. The teacher will apply strategies and techniques for structuring a variety of classroom interactions.

3. The teacher will promote metacognition through modeling his/her own thinking process and helping students become aware of their own thinking.

4. The teacher will provide for explicit instruction of thinking skills.

The Thinking Skills Resource Book is a compilation of creative and critical thinking skills which can be used in the classroom. Material has been developed for each skill which contains the information a teacher needs to plan lessons to introduce the specific skill, provide guided practice and allow students to apply the skill. Each skill should be the focus of five to eight lessons in order to develop the skill for transfer and application.

It is suggested that a scope and sequence of thinking skills be developed to insure systematic instruction in a curriculum for thinking. A sample scope and sequence for grades K-5 is provided in the appendix. Barry Beyer states that every school system "should have a comprehensive program that teaches thinking skills systematically and directly to all students throughout the curriculum."

While it is suggested that the steps within the process lesson format be followed, the applications to content areas are merely suggestions. The Thinking Skills Resource Book is a guide for you to adapt as best suits your class.

SEQUENCE OF A PROCESS SKILL LESSON

Based on Madeline Hunter's
Instructional Theory Into Practice

1.0   **Anticipatory Set**

2.0   **Objective and Purpose**

      2.1   Name the skill.
      2.2   Define the skill in language appropriate to the grade level of the student.
      2.3   Give examples of skill in use.

3.0   **Input**

      3.1   Explain the skill.
      3.2   Do a concrete example.

4.0   **Model the Skill**

      4.1   Lead the students through the skill step by step.
      4.2   Refer to the steps as you move through the skill.
      4.3   Teach thinking out loud.

5.0   **Check for Understanding**

6.0   **Guided Practice**

      6.1   Students engage in the skill—practice with teacher guidance on life experiences or previously learned content.
      6.2   Repeat this practice as often as necessary.
      6.3   Provide feedback to students on the product obtained.
      6.4   Allow time for students to discuss the skill and their work with it.

7.0   **Closure**

      7.1   Review steps of the skill.
      7.2   Examine products of the skill.

8.0   **Independent Practice**

      8.1   Discuss transfer to new areas.
      8.2   Offer practice of skill in new areas.

THINKING SKILLS

RESOURCE BOOK

Lorene Reid

CREATIVE THINKING SKILLS

To the Teacher:

Creative thinking is defined by Costa as "the act of being able to produce along new and original lines" (Costa, 1985). Students of today will be involved in careers and experiences which will require the use of creative problem solving skills. Research indicates that an individual's creative abilities can be developed through systematic training. We teach for creative thinking so that students will be producers of knowledge rather than consumers of knowledge. Teaching the skills of creative thinking will encourage divergent thinking abilities, the use of higher level thought processes and the development of a variety of talents.

The following section provides the necessary information to organize skill lessons. Lessons are designed to teach the basic process skills identified in creative thinking and problem solving. The teacher should use the material to plan explicit instruction in the techniques of creative thinking. The activities are designed to encourage divergent thinking, create an environment in which thinking can occur and enhance the creative process. Use the ideas that are suggested or be creative and develop your own application when transferring skill to content.

FLUENCY

DEFINITION	Fluency is the generation of many responses, solutions to a problem, answers to a question, possibilities, or consequences. Being fluent is being able to think of many ideas.
OBJECTIVE AND PURPOSE	Fluency is taught as a technique to develop a method for listing a large number of options to consider or evaluate.

PROVIDING INFORMATION

Guidelines:

1. Large number of responses is wanted.
2. There is no correct number of answers.
3. Skill is done orally.
4. One person speaks at a time.
5. All responses are accepted.

Model Skill:

Use such topics as the following:

- List ways to spend your allowance.
- List things you could make from a mailbox.
- List things that are blue.
- List things that come in threes.

Guided Practice:

Use such topics as the following:

- Name things that fall.
- List reasons for not cleaning your room.
- List things to do with a newspaper.

INDEPENDENT PRACTICE

Language Arts
- List words or phrases to describe a rainy day.
- List things that begin with "m."

Math
- Name ways to measure time.
- List all the things that are round or square, etc.

Science
- Name things that are sweet.
- List words that are related to space.

Social Studies
- List words that describe school.
- List things that your family could do on the weekend.

FLEXIBILITY

DEFINITION	Flexibility is the ability to think of alternatives to a problem or situation. Being flexible means to change your direction of thinking and adapt to different situations.
OBJECTIVE AND PURPOSE	Flexibility is taught as a technique for developing a number of options from a variety of approaches.

PROVIDING INFORMATION

Guidelines:

1. Explain the difference between fluency and flexibility.
2. State topic or concern.
3. Take time to examine many possibilities.
4. Encourage flexibility by asking, "What other ways?" "What different kinds?" "Suppose that..."
5. Use your five senses: How would it feel, taste, look, etc.?

Model Skill:

Use a topic such as animals. Do your thinking orally so students can follow your progress as you change categories.

Guided Practice:

Use such ideas as the following:
- In what different ways could we use a comb?
- What could you find in a messy room?
- What are some uses for an old tire?

INDEPENDENT PRACTICE

Language Arts

- How many words can you list that would replace the word *said*?
- Select a fairy tale and come up with new ways for the main character to solve his or her problem.

Math

- List things that we can measure.
- Name things that are square.

Science

- List many terms related to space.
- Think of many places a butterfly could hide to get away from the rain.

Social Studies

- List many problems of a President of the United States.
- List words associated with Thanksgiving.

ORIGINALITY

DEFINITION	Originality is the ability to think of new or unusual ideas or products; going beyond the common or obvious answers.
OBJECTIVE AND PURPOSE	Original thinkers search for new ideas, new approaches and novel, unique solutions to problems. An original thinker continues to develop divergent thinking abilities. New inventions depend on original ideas.

PROVIDING INFORMATION

Guidelines:

1. Reinforce the idea of originality—no rephrasing of someone else's ideas.
2. Encourage students to generate many ideas before selecting their last response.
3. Review use of fluency and flexibility.

Model Skill:

- Imagine that you are twenty feet tall. Discuss: What would you use for a hat? shoes? bathtub? plate? house? pet?

- If your book could talk to you, what would it say?

Guided Practice:

- Create a new candy bar that would appeal to students your age. Make it delicious and attractive. Design a wrapper which will attract shoppers attention.

- Design logos for a rock star, a government official, the principal of your school, yourself, etc.

- Combine a paper plate, paper napkins, a plastic fork and spoon, drinking straws, and paper clips to form a new invention. Name your product and describe its uses.

INDEPENDENT PRACTICE

Language Arts

- Develop a new ending for a favorite story.
- Create a new alphabet.

Math

- Pick your favorite number and describe or illustrate it in an unusual way.
- Create an unusual design using the geometric shape of a triangle.

Science

- Describe a new animal. Decide where the animal lives, what it eats, and the advantages and disadvantages to humans.
- Design original experiments to explain conditions for plant growth.

Social Studies

- Design an underwater home.
- Create a new board game for people to play.

ELABORATION

DEFINITION	Elaboration is the process of expanding an idea or product by adding details.
OBJECTIVE AND PURPOSE	Elaboration is used to make an idea or product more detailed or interesting. It is the process of exploring alternatives to enhance an idea or to make a product more complete.

PROVIDING INFORMATION

Guidelines:

1. Examine the idea or product to be used.
2. Decide on the main idea.
3. Decide what details could be added to embellish the idea.
4. Add appropriate details.

Statements to help students elaborate:
- What can you add to make _____ better?
- Enlarge _____.
- Draw a square on the board. Have students elaborate on the figure one at a time.

Model Skill:

Use any of the following to model the skill:
- Add details to a map to make direction clearer.
- Elaborate on the sentence one word at a time: The dog ran.
- Elaborate on a glass, straw, paper clip, etc. to make it more useful or fun to use.

Guided Practice:

- Design a playground for our school.
- Build a habitat for your pet mouse.
- Expand or embellish any of the following familiar objects: milk carton, paper bag, telephone, or bar of soap.

INDEPENDENT PRACTICE

Language Arts

- Write a story. Elaborate on your idea by illustrating the story.
- Create a new character for a familiar story. Rewrite the story, adding this new person.
- Tall tales are excellent examples of elaboration. Create your own tall tale.

Math

- Add on the equations to make different equations for the same number (i.e. 3+3=6, 1+3+3-1=6).

Science

- Collect words from magazines and newspapers which would elaborate on a concept such as temperture.
- Add different variables to an experiment and test those results.

Social Studies

- Elaborate on an event in history that is familiar to the students.
- Design a seal for your city or school.

BRAINSTORMING

DEFINITION

Brainstorming combines the techniques of flexibility, fluency, originality and elaboration to produce a large quantity of ideas in a group setting where shared ideas inspire new ones.

OBJECTIVE AND PURPOSE

Brainstorming is used to generate many varied ideas, solutions, or responses. From a quantity of ideas there will be more choices for evaluation. Students learn the valuable skill of deferred judgment.

PROVIDING INFORMATION

Guidelines:

1. Criticism is ruled out—accept all responses.
2. Free-wheeling is welcomed—not all responses will be of high quality.
3. Combine and improve on ideas. Encourage hitchhiking on each other's ideas.
4. Quantity is wanted. The goal is to produce many responses.

Model Skill:

Divide the class into teams. Select one team to work with you. Act as the group leader. Call on one person at a time and record all ideas. Brainstorm ideas on topics such as "things that are red."

Guided Practice:

Use such ideas as
- Excuses to explain why homework isn't done.
- Ways to remove snow without shoveling it.
- What are some disadvantages of living in a straw house?
- What would be interesting to find out about a/an _____?

INDEPENDENT PRACTICE

Language Arts

- Brainstorm a list of words used to describe a character in a story.
- List words that gave the long *O* sound.

Math

- List things that come in pairs.
- Write down as many multiplication problems as you can which have a 2 in the answer.

Science

- List ways to save endangered animals.
- How can we solve the problem of getting rid of fast food containers?

Social Studies

- Think of something boring and make it interesting.
- In what ways might we improve our classroom, school, community, etc.

MODIFICATION

DEFINITION

Modification is a method used to enhance the creative thinking process by using a series of idea gathering techniques called SCAMPER. The process of creative imagination is one of rearranging or manipulating information that is in the form of knowledge or experience.

OBJECTIVE AND PURPOSE

Modification is a technique used to improve imaginative talent. The checklist of SCAMPER contains questions or suggestions that stimulate an individual to form creative ideas. Children will have the opportunity to learn and practice techniques used by authors, inventors, business, a n d i n - dustry. SCAMPER is taken from the "Idea Spurring Checklist" developed by Alex Osborn (Eberle, 1971).

PROVIDING INFORMATION

The SCAMPER technique uses the following idea stimulations:

S	Substitute	Who or what else? Other materials, processes, ingredients?
C	Combine	Put together new ideas, purposes, uses, characteristics.
A	Adapt	Adapt to suit another purpose. What other ideas does this suggest?
M	Modify	Change the color, form, shape, motion, sound.
P	Put to other uses	New ways to use as it is or modified.
E	Eliminate	To remove, omit, or get rid of a quality.
R	Rearrange	To adjust, move, alter, transpose.
	Reverse	To turn it around, think about opposites, turn it upside down.

REMEMBER   Defer all judgment on ideas produced while you are involved in the idea gathering process.

Model Skill:

- Students generate an initial list of ideas for a family vacation.
- Use SCAMPER techniques to improve on the ideas. It is a good idea to have these techniques written out.

Guided Practice:

- Design a new playground for the school.
- Improve the school cafeteria.
- Plan a birthday party for a friend.

MODIFICATION (continued)

INDEPENDENT PRACTICE

Language Arts
- Rewrite a story such as "Jack and the Beanstalk" so that the giant is a kind and generous hero.
- Invent a new kind of sandwich.

Math
- How could we improve the math textbook?
- Add a thirteenth month to the calendar. Give it a name, holidays, and a season that it will be in.

Science
- Create new zoo animals. Name them based on their characteristics.
- Design a space colony.

Social Studies
- Select any tool, utensil or machine and improve it.
- Given an outline map of the school, ask students to improve on the information given.

CURIOSITY

DEFINITION	Curiosity is the ability to wonder, ponder or puzzle. A curious person wants to find answers to questions, to investigate, to find out what will happen.
OBJECTIVE AND PURPOSE	Curiosity is the quality that motivates students to learn more, to ask why, what if...

PROVIDING INFORMATION

Guidelines: Show you are curious by asking questions, wanting to know what will happen or following a hunch.

Model Skill:
- Display a picture or bring in a real tool that would not be familiar.
- Orally ask questions about the particular item and list them for students to see.

Guided Practice:
- Why shouldn't the sun shine all the time?
- What if you couldn't go to school?
- Why are plants important?

INDEPENDENT PRACTICE

Language Arts
- Discuss why an author used a particular style in writing.
- Stop reading a story and discuss what would happen if...

Math
- Discuss what would happen if numbers on pages of a book got mixed up.

Science
- Why does a plant need sunlight?
- What would happen to an experiment if we changed one of the substances.

Social Studies
- Discuss why we need certain jobs in each community. What if there were no policemen?
- Why do we need certain rules for the playground?

IMAGERY

People use their imagination to predict solutions to a problem. Inventors use their imagination to visualize how a new product might work; artists to create a work of art.

DEFINITION
Imagery is picturing something or building a mental image to look into the future, to bring the past back to life or to invent new things.

OBJECTIVE AND PURPOSE
Imagination is used to reach beyond real boundaries. It is an essential tool of human intelligence.

PROVIDING INFORMATION

Guidelines:
1. Use imagery and fantasy to stretch your imagination.
2. Use your five senses to help you imagine.
3. Put no limits or boundaries on your imagining.
4. Try to become that object or person.
5. Generate many ideas. (fluency)

Model Skill:
Use a picture of people or an animal. Discuss orally questions such as the following:
- What are they doing? Why?
- Where are they?
- How do they feel?
- What has happened?
- What will happen next?

Guided Practice:
- What might you see if you were a kite?
- Imagine you are a mouse in a corner during a Valentine party.
- Describe living in outer space.

INDEPENDENT PRACTICE

Language Arts
- Make up a new character who would come at Christmas.
- Create an ending to an unfinished story or rewrite an ending to a story you know.

Math
- Imagine numbers could talk. What would they say?
- Picture one hundred pennies, then one thousand, one million, one billion.

Science
- Imagine you are an insect being chased by a frog. Think how you would feel. Visualize what you might do to get away.
- Imagine you could invent a new car that does not run on gasoline. What would it look like?

Social Studies
- Imagine you lived in George Washington's time. Describe what you might see.
- What changes would you like to see in the world?

ASSOCIATIVE THINKING

DEFINITION

Associative thinking describes a common element or connection between ideas, objects, concepts or events.

OBJECTIVE AND PURPOSE

To develop and extend critical thinking skills.

PROVIDING INFORMATION

Guidelines:

1. Identify basic attributes of one set of ideas, objects, or concepts.
2. Identify attributes which are common to both groups.

   Use: _____ is/are alike _____ because _____.

Model Skill:

- Use mystery box with a collection of objects which students describe as they touch them—round like a ball, soft like cotton.

Guided Practice:

- Use book *Q is for Duck, and Alphabet Guessing Game* by May Etting and Michael Folson, Clarion Books/Ticknor & Fields, a Houghton Mifflin Company.
- A is for zoo. Why? Because animals live in the zoo.
- Describe famous pairs such as bread and _____, salt and_____.

INDEPENDENT PRACTICE

Language Arts

- Complete simple similies.
- Choose a letter of the alphabet and draw pictures of words associated with that letter.

Math

- Name ways we use math every day.
- How are numbers like a road map?

Science

- Select a broad topic like desert, space or water, and list terms we associate with that topic.

Social Studies

- Students observe a picture of an old invention and then describe the object and its use and associate it with a familiar invention.

CREATIVE PROBLEM SOLVING

DEFINITION

Creative Problem Solving is a six-step process used to solve a problem in an imaginative way. The result of this systematic procedure is an effective plan of action.

OBJECTIVE AND PURPOSE

Creative Problem Solving involves use of brainstorming techniques at each step to increase the possibility of finding a better solution. This process has been adapted for use by children (Noller, Parnes, and Biondi, 1976).

PROVIDING INFORMATION

Guidelines:

1. Mess Finding—Identify the problem.
2. Fact Finding—Gather as much information about the problem as you can: who, what, where, when, how.
3. Problem Finding—Identify sub-problems and write as problem statement. Select a specific, manageable problem and write in problem form: In what ways might I?
4. Idea Finding—Gather ideas for solution to the problem.
5. Solution Finding/Evaluation—Judge possible solutions according to criteria.
6. Acceptance Finding—Decide on a plan of action for putting solution into effect.

Model Skill:

You and your friends are planning a surprise party for one of your friends. At lunch time, your friend announces that he is going on a trip with his parents and will be leaving on the day you have planned the party. What will you do?

1. What important facts can you state about the situation?

2. State the major problem.

3. List ways to solve the problem.

4. Select your five best ideas and enter on a decision grid.

CRITERIA

Best Ideas	Can I Do It?	Will It Work?	Your Criteria	TOTAL

CREATIVE PROBLEM SOLVING (continued)

5. Evaluate each idea on a scale of 1-5. A high rating is 5, a low rating is 1.
6. Total the score for each idea.
7. The best solution is_____.

Guided Practice: Use such ideas as the following:
- A younger brother or sister who gets into your things, messes them up, and often breaks your possessions.
- Problems with waste in the lunchroom.

INDEPENDENT PRACTICE

Language Arts
- Choose any problem encountered in a story and use the process to create a solution.
- How does your solution compare with the author's solution?

Math
- Use the Creative Problem Solving process to arrive at a solution for helping students learn math facts.

Science
- Use problems such as endangered species, acid rain, and pollution to encourage research and use the Creative Problem Solving process to discuss alternatives and solutions.

Social Studies
- Problems dealing with society such as unemployment, the elderly, illiteracy.

ATTRIBUTE LISTING

DEFINITION

To generate many ideas about an object or solutions to a problem by looking closely at the attributes or characteristics.

OBJECTIVE AND PURPOSE

Attribute listing is used in problem solving. Analysis is required to separate data by looking at various attributes. Synthesis is used to improve ideas.

PROVIDING INFORMATION

Guidelines:

1. List component parts of a given solution or problem.
2. Find and list major characteristics-attributes of each component (physical, social, economic).
3. Find and list major attributes of each component.
4. Brainstorm and elaborate improvements—combinations/ alternatives for each attribute.

Model Skill:

- Discuss how we can describe things: color, size, shape, use, taste, texture, etc.

1. List attributes of *ice cream:*: cold, sweet, low cost, makes me feel good to eat.
2. What else has similar attributes?
3. Combine - ice cream and milk - milkshake.

Guided Practice:

- Use chart form such as the one below to help students organize data.

How could we make a garage more useful? List attributes.

Improving a Garage		
Components	*Attributes*	*Improvement*
Walls Floor	Open beams Poured cement	Paint Panel Drop ceiling Heat

Combine to create a workshop.

- Select an object such as a wastebasket, spoon or vacuum cleaner. List the attributes of the object. What else has similar attributes? How could they be combined to develop a new product?
- Choose two verbs such as rolling and falling.

Rolling	*Falling*
skates	child

ATTRIBUTE LISTING (continued)

Combine ideas to invent a padded roller skating rink.

INDEPENDENT PRACTICE

Language Arts
- List attributes of a character in a story.
- Write a paragraph describing the person by the attributes you listed.
- Analyze attributes of a good mystery story.

Math
- Solve word problems.

Science
- Analyze important characteristics of an ecosystem.
- What factors influence invention or discovery.

SYNECTICS OR METAPHORICAL THINKING

DEFINITION

Metaphorical thinking is seeing a relationship between two "unlike" things, people, animals, objects, events or concepts—the joining of different and seemingly irrelevant elements.

OBJECTIVE AND PURPOSE

Synectics, or thinking in metaphors, involves creative thinking. The student goes beyond the obvious to seek a unique relationship. Synectics methods can be materials for lessons on creative thinking techniques and the importance of metephorical thinking in creativity and finding new ideas and inventions.

PROVIDING INFORMATION

Guidelines:

1. Observe. Look for the interesting, unusual, different in each part of the metaphor.
2. Define basic attributes of things being observed.
3. Define basic attributes of each part of the metaphor.
4. Compare. How are the attributes alike; different?
5. Complete the following: _____ is like _____ because _____.

Model Skill:

- How is the ocean like the sky?
- Which is softer, a pillow or a lap? Why?
- A doughnut is like a _____ because_____.

Guided Practice:

- Why is a ice like a mirror?
- When you are angry, you are like a _____.
- Which vegetable is most like you? Why?

INDEPENDENT PRACTICE

Language Arts

- Create cartoon strips that are metaphorical based on news events, popular movies, etc.

Math

- Fractions are like _____ because_____.
- Try attribute listing to compare two ways of doing things.

Science

- A parachute is like what animal? Why?
- What would it be like to be inside a pumpkin?

Social Studies

- What could have given Thomas Edison the idea for a lightbulb? What was the connection?
- How are styles of today like the 1960s?

FORCED RELATIONSHIPS

DEFINITION

A forced relationship creates a relationship between the attribute characteristics or dimensions of two or more seemingly unrelated items, concepts, or ideas to find a previously unimagined idea or solution.

OBJECTIVE AND PURPOSE

Through the combination of unrelated items or ideas, new inventions, products, or concepts can be developed. Forced relationship is a technique of creative thinking. It is effective when students reach a _____ in brainstorming, as it can increase the number of previously unimagined ideas.

PROVIDING INFORMATION

Guidelines:

There are two types of forced relationship processes.

1. Lists. Randomly placed words in two lists. Select one word from one list and one from the other list and try to relate them in new ways.
2. Fixed. One object is fixed while selection occurs from other randomly selected words in a list. Relate the one to the others in some new way.

For example: Chair   Buttons
Snow
Refrigerator
Lunch Box

Steps:

1. Review the skill of association with students.
2. Have them brainstorm words associated with the first word, then the second.
3. Compare the lists to decide on a forced relationship.
4. Provide a logical explanation for the chosen relationship. There is no correct answer.

Model Skill:

• How is a piano like a woodpecker?

Piano	*Woodpecker*
instrument	bird
non-living	living
keys	lives in tree
play	sing
black and white	black and white
made from a tree	

Both a piano and a bird make music.

FORCED RELATIONSHIPS (continued)

Guided Practice:	• Which flower is most like you?
	• How is sadness like a stomach ache?
	• How are a book and a television alike?

INDEPENDENT PRACTICE

Language Arts	• Take two characters from different stories and combine them into one story.
Math	• How is a number line like a railroad track?
Science	• How is a straw like a stream?
Social Studies	• How is freedom like a fox?

CREATIVE THINKING PROCESS

DEFINITION

Creative thinking is a set of steps or stages through which a creative person proceeds to arrive at a new idea, solution, or product.

OBJECTIVE AND PURPOSE

Students will be made aware of the stages that occur in creative thinking and recognize that creative thinking takes time. The techniques they have learned can be applied to the process of creative thinking.

PROVIDING INFORMATION

Guidelines:

The four stages in the creative process based on the Wallas model (1926) are

Preparation: Gathering data and information as a background for clarifying the problem.

Incubation: Taking time to reflect, allowing the unconscious to rise to the surface.

Illumination: The "Aha! I've found it!" stage in which a solution appears.

Verification: Checking or testing the idea to see if it really works.

Creative attitudes include tha following:

1. An awareness of creativity and its importance.
2. Thinking creatively instead of doing things the same way.
3. The belief that everyone can be more creative with a little effort.
4. Being receptive to creative ideas of others (Davis p. 87).

Model Skill:

- Use the writing process in which you are given an assignment to write a paragraph about friendship.

Preparation: Brainstorm attributes of a friend.

Incubation: Discuss time involved in selection of the best idea. Test several ideas.

Illumination: Choice is made.

Verification: First draft is written.

Guided Practice:

- Write ads for the help wanted section of the newspaper.
- Use a cartoon strip to describe a new invention such as a device to assist in water conservation.
- Transform a known invention from its intended use to a new or alternative use, for example, a perfume atomizer or a tape recorder.

CREATIVE THINKING PROCESS (continued)

INDEPENDENT PRACTICE

Language Arts
- Collect newspaper headlines. Students can write the story.
- Write a story on any assigned topic.

Math
- Develop an easier way to teach a math process.
- Devise new ways for computers to help us in school.

Science
- Create a machine which will clean your room.
- Design a car which will operate with an alternative energy source.

Social Studies
- Design a new type of school building in which students might be able to learn better.
- Create a new leader or person who will be famous in history.

REFERENCES

Clements, S., & Kolbe, K. Villapando E. (1983). *Do-It-Yourself Critical and Creative Thinking.* Phoenix, Arizona: Kathy Kolbe Concept, Inc.

Eberle, B. & Stanish B. (1985). *CPS for Kids.* E. Aurora, New York: D.O.K. Publishers.

Eberle, R. (1987). *Scamper.* East Aurora, New York: D.O.K. Publishers.

Flack, J. (1985). *Once Upon a Time.* East Aurora, New York: D.O.K. Publishers.

Jaffe, C. *On the Road to Creativity.* Buffalo, New York: D.O.K. Publishers.

Muncy, P. (1985). *Springboards to Creative Thinking.* West Nyack, New York: The Center for Applied Research in Education, Inc.

Polette, N. (1987). *The ABC's of Books and Thinking Skills.* O'Fallon, Missouri: Book Lures, Inc.

Ricca, J. & Treffinger, D. (1982). *Adventures in Creative Thinking.* Buffalo, New York: D.O.K. Publishers.

Stanish, B. & Eberle, B. (1984). *Be a Problem Solver.* East Aurora, New York: D.O. K. Publishers.

Stanish, B. (1979). *I Believe in Unicorns.* Carthage, Illinois: Good Apple, Inc.

Stanish, B. (1981). *The Unconventional Invention Book.* Carthage, Illinois: Good Apple, Inc.

Swartz, L. (1984). *Creative Capers.* Santa Barbara, California: The Learning Works.

Wellner, B. & Yoder J. (1985). *Productive Thinking and Planning.* East Aurora, New York: D.O.K. Publishers.

CRITICAL THINKING SKILLS

To the Teacher:

Critical thinking is a persistent effort to examine evidence which supports any belief, solution, or conclusion prior to its acceptance. The ability to think clearly and reason logically is a primary goal of education.

TWELVE ASPECTS OF CRITICAL THINKING

1. Grasp the meaning of a statement.

2. Judge whether abiguity exists.

3. Judge if contradictions exist.

4. Judge if a conclusion necessarily follows.

5. Judge the specificity of a statement.

6. Judge if a statement relates to a certain principle.

7. Judge the reliability of an observation.

8. Judge if an inductive conclusion is warranted.

9. Judge if a problem has been identified.

10. Judge if a definition is adequate.

11. Judge if a statement is credible.

12. Judge if something is an assumption.

REFERENCE: Ennis, Robert H., "A Critical Concept of Critical Thinking," *Harvard Review*, Vol. 32, Nol. 1, Winter 1962.

The following lessons are designed to provide the information necessary to teach basic process skills that apply to critical and logical thinking. The teacher should use the material to plan lessons for explicit instruction in each skill. Use familiar content to introduce the thinking skill, then teach for transfer of skill to content.

CLASSIFICATION

DEFINITION	Classification is the organization of items or concepts by characteristics, uses or relationships.
OBJECTIVE AND PURPOSE	Classification is taught to help students organize data into a defined meaningful structure.

PROVIDING INFORMATION

Guidelines:

1. Examine all items to identify characteristics.
2. Select a basis for grouping.
3. Sort items according to the feature(s) they share.
4. Name the groupings based on the common features.
5. Justify the items in your group.

There may be more than one way to classify objects.

Model Skills

- Use a box of buttons. Orally demonstrate the thinking you are doing as you examine the buttons for common features. Begin to sort buttons based on stated criteria. Give each group a name. Justify items in each grouping.

Guided Practice:

- Give students an assortment of rocks to classify.
- Bring in a bag of items such as hats and have students classify the items.
- Classify a collection of animal pictures.

INDEPENDENT PRACTICE

Language Arts

- Classify characters from fairy tales.
- Classify story titles from a reading book.

Math

- Classify numbers from 0-9.
- Classify a variety of geometric shapes.

Science

- Classify animals according to what they eat.
- Group a list of common items into living and non-living groups.

Social Studies

- Classify a random list of methods of transportation.
- Classify a variety of occupations.

COMPARISON

DEFINITION	Comparison is the skill of looking closely at items to discover likenesses and differences.
OBJECTIVE AND PURPOSE	The comparison of items to determine likenesses and differences is a basis for observation and classification. Comparison helps students see relationships.

PROVIDING INFORMATION

Guidelines:
1. Examine objects to be compared.
2. Identify all the ways they are alike.
3. Identify ways in which they are different.
4. Describe the similarities and differences.
5. Summarize and draw conclusions from your identification of like/unlike qualities.

Model Skill:
- Display an apple and an orange.
- Orally identify all the qualities shared.
- Orally identify all the qualities which are different (practice attribue listing).
- Draw conclusions.

Guided Practice:
- Compare cats and dogs.
- Compare popcorn and potato chips.
- Compare snowballs and ice cubes.

INDEPENDENT PRACTICE

Language Arts
- Compare two fairy tales.
- Compare characters in a story.

Math
- Compare geometric shapes.
- Compare money.

Science
- Compare two or more rocks.
- Compare two or more plants.

Social Studies
- Compare jobs of various community helpers.
- Compare apartment buildings and houses.

PATTERNING

DEFINITION

Patterning is discovering an expected route, movement, or arrangement of parts. Patterning is an integral part of problem solving.

OBJECTIVE AND PURPOSE

By exploring and recognizing patterns that are a part of daily life, students will look for patterns that may help find answers in a problem solving situation.

PROVIDING INFORMATION

Guidelines:

1. Examine existing information to determine the pattern.
2. State the rule.
3. Determine if the rule is correct by continuing the pattern.

Model Skill:

Use colored cubes or beads to set up patterns such as the following:
- Red, green, blue, red, green, _____.
- What will come next? Red, red, green, red, _____? (red)
- Orally discuss how you are thinking.

Guided Practice:

- Provide children with a variety of concrete patterns with sizes, shapes, and colors for them to predict what will come next.

INDEPENDENT PRACTICE

Language Arts

- Use nursery rhymes to predict word patterns.
- Use alphabet patterns such as a, c, e, to predict what letter will come next.

Math

- Use number patterns to predict what number will come next, for example: 2, 4, 6, 8, ____.

Science

- Use life cycles to predict the next developmental stage.
- Use seasons of the year to determine what season will follow.

Social Studies

- Identify patterns involved in making a phone call to determine what will come next.
- Discuss patterns involved in everyday events such as getting ready for school, putting on shoes and socks.

SEQUENCING

DEFINITION	Sequencing is placing items, processes, etc. in a logical order.
OBJECTIVE AND PURPOSE	Sequencing helps students organize ideas or processes into a structure that makes sense. Sequencing is an important skill in developing a plan of action.

PROVIDING INFORMATION

Guidelines:

1. Identify the purpose, goal, or end result for sequencing.
2. Decide which items, processes, etc. are first and last.
3. Arrange remaining items in the correct order.
4. Check to see if any steps or items were left out.
5. Evaluate the final arrangement to determine if it makes sense.

Model Skill:

- Display random order of steps in making a cake.
- Read orally through the list to determine the purpose.
- Find first and last step. Tell why.
- Arrange the remaining steps between first and last.
- Check to see if any items were left out.
- See if final arrangement makes sense.

Guided Practice:

- Put a picture story in order.
- Ordering objects—smallest to largest, fastest to slowest, and so on.
- How to make, build, do a _____ . (For example, peanut butter and jelly sandwich.)

INDEPENDENT PRACTICE

Language Arts

- Write or give directions on doing a task in order.
- Arrange parts of a story in order.

Math

- Arrange numbers in order (smallest to largest or the reverse).
- Arrange money according to worth.

Science

- Arrange animals, plant, planets according to size.
- List steps involved in growing a garden.

Social Studies

- Arrange dates from earliest to most recent.
- Use time lines to sequence events.

CAUSE AND EFFECT

DEFINITION	Cause and effect describes the relationship between two events in which one event causes another event to happen.
OBJECTIVE AND PURPOSE	Cause and effect is a Critical Thinking skill which gives students the understanding that one action may result in another action. Students will develop an understanding of the consequences of their behavior.

PROVIDING INFORMATION

Guidelines:
- The *effect* tells what happens.
- The *cause* tells the reason it happened.
- Look for the causes first if the lesson asks, "What are the effects?"
- Look for the effects first if the lesson asks, "What are the causes?"
- If both cause and effect are asked for, it is helpful to set up a chart to identify both.

Model Skill: Always review explanations of cause and effect before each lesson. Use such topics as
- What could be the causes of your TV not working?
- Why were we late for the movie?
- What could be causes for a child crying?
- What could be the effects of tripping over a rock?

Guided Practice: What would be the causes and effects of
- no paper in the classroom?
- a noisy classroom?
- not getting to school on time?

INDEPENDENT PRACTICE

Language Arts
- Select a situation from a book. Examine the causes and effects.
- What are the causes and effects of illiteracy?

Math
- Examine causes and effects of poor math grades.
- What are the causes and effects of spending too much money?

Science
- What would be the causes and effects of wasting water?
- What are the effects of electricity on our lives?

Social Studies
- Examine causes and effects of a traffic tie up.
- Discuss causes and effects of any current event.

LABELING

DEFINITION   Labeling affixes a name to an item. Labeling connects a word with a mental image; it requires classification and naming.

OBJECTIVE AND PURPOSE   Labeling is important to students as a strategy to build their vocabulary. A strong vocabulary is an important first step in helping students acquire thinking skills.

PROVIDING INFORMATION

Guidelines:
1. Examine items to be named or labeled.
2. Seek familiar patterns.
3. Label from general to specific (i.e. from tree to oak tree).
4. Pair the word or label with its image.

Model Skill:
- Select a picture with several items and orally demonstrate how you would label the items. Discuss ways to group the item listed.

Guided Practice:
- Provide students with a variety of pictures which could be labeled.

INDEPENDENT PRACTICE

Language Arts
- Label all items that begin with a certain sound ("b") in a picture.
- Collect pictures and label each for a dictionary.

Math
- Label shapes for a bulletin board design.
- Label sets of items with both name and number.

Science
- Label simple machines.
- Label parts of the human body.

Social Studies
- Label items found on a map.
- Label members of a family or a family tree.

OBSERVATION

DEFINITION	Observation is the skill of examining objects or events carefully through the use of the five senses.
OBJECTIVE AND PURPOSE	Observation is a fundamental thinking skill as it underlies and supports other identification skills. Observation is an important technique for gathering information.

PROVIDING INFORMATION

Guidelines:
- You may only describe information obtained by using your senses. In other words, no assumptions or inferences should be made.
- Describe a steak cooking on a grill.

Model Skill:
- Identify a peach using five senses. How do your senses help you to know that this is a peach?

Apply Skill:
- Students use the outdoors to observe and record information about a tree.
- Students observe a peanut and then identify their peanut from a group of peanuts.
- How would you know you were in the following places if you could not see: gym, classroom, cafeteria, zoo, factory.

Review the definition of observation and reasons for careful observation.

INDEPENDENT PRACTICE

Language Arts
- Look for descriptive words in a paragraph that paint a mental image.
- Observe a picture and describe the objects that are seen.

Math
- Examine pictures of buildings to find various geometric shapes. Use graphs to gather information.

Science
- Science experiments to observe and record sequence of events, effects of change. For example: How does the temperature of water affect the breathing rate of fish?
- Use senses to describe likenesses and differences of sugar, salt, cornstarch, and flour.

Social Studies
- Gather information from a picture. For example, what does this picture tell you about the living conditions of inhabitants of this place?

WEBBING

DEFINITION   Webbing is a method of organizing thoughts into subtopics and details which support a main idea or topic.

OBJECTIVE AND PURPOSE   To organize random thoughts or images into a diagram. Webbing is an introduction to formal outlining.

PROVIDING INFORMATION

Guidelines:
1. Main topic is written in the center of the web.
2. Subtopics are shown as spokes coming out of the center.
3. Skill of classification is reviewed in order to help students obtain the needed subtopics and details.
4. Details are shown in smaller boxes.
5. Subtopics are related to the main idea and details support the subtopic.
6. There are no correct number of subtopics or details for each main idea.

Model Skill:
• Model the skill of webbing by doing a description of school.

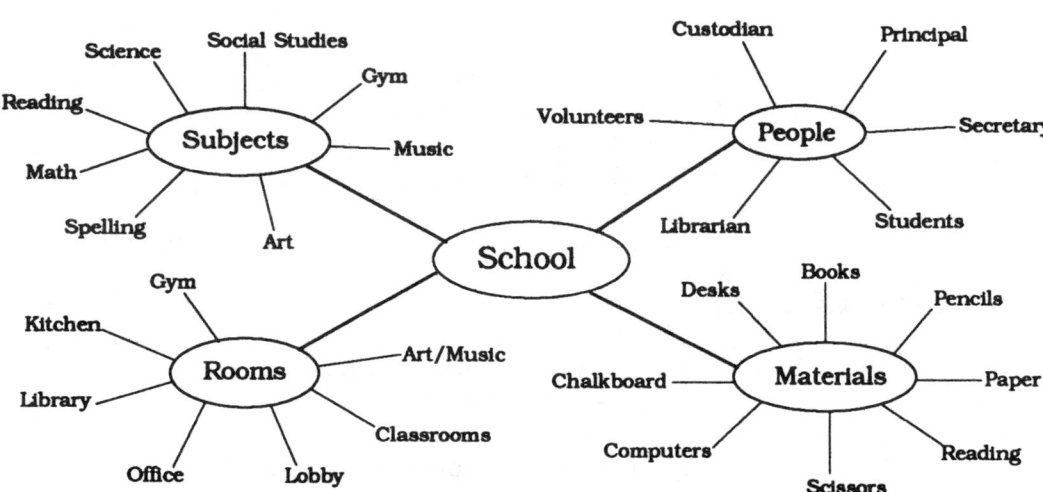

Guided Practice:
• Students construct a web of ideas for writing about a season of the year.

INDEPENDENT PRACTICE

Webbing can be used in all subject areas. It can be used to organize ideas prior to a writing assignment, as a chapter review or planning an activity. Webbing is an excellent tool for understanding literary elements.

LOGICAL THINKING

DEFINITION

"Logical reasoning is thinking in a systematic fashion in order to determine the truth or validity of an argument." (Costa, p. 311).

OBJECTIVE AND PURPOSE

Strategies of logic are taught to enable students to reach conclusions that are valid. Formal logic includes the principles of inductive and deductive reasoning

Inductive reasoning requires the student to reach a conclusion based on reasoning from the specific to the general. Examples include reasoning by analogy or explaining why.

Deductive reasoning requires the student to reach a conclusion based on reasoning from the general to the specific. Examples of this type of reasoning are categorical, syllogisms, and hypothetical.

The following skills are introduced to students:

1.0 Solving Analogies

2.0 Syllogisms

    2.1   All statements
    2.2   No statements
    2.3   If _____ then _____
    2.4   Reversing rules of logic

3.0 Organizing Information to Solve Problems

PROVIDING INFORMATION

Guidelines:

1. Begin with assumption or purpose.
2. Generate step-by-step orders.
3. Arrive at a conclusion.
4. Determine if conclusion is valid.

CATEGORICAL SYLLOGISMS

DEFINITION

An inference is made from the relationship of two statements to a third statement.

An **All Statement** is a statement that is true for all members of a group. If the statement is true for the group as a whole it is true for all members of the group. All Statements cannot be reversed and still be valid.

A **No Statement** begins with the word *no*. No Statements can be reversed and still be true.

OBJECTIVE AND PURPOSE

Students will be able to draw conclusions based on previously acquired knowledge.

PROVIDING INFORMATION—ALL STATEMENTS

Use the following example to explain All Statements:
- All cats were once kittens. Puff is a cat. So we know Puff was a kitten.
- Blackie is a cat. So we know Blackie was once a kitten.

Model Skill:

Use such examples as the following:
- All airplanes fly. A jet is an airplane. So we know a jet _____.
- All triangles have three sides. The drawing has the shape of a triangle. So we know that the drawing _____.

Guided Practice:

Provide examples for students to solve:
- All butterflies are insects. An insect has six legs. So we know that a butterfly_____.

- All third graders are students. Susan is in third grade. So we know Susan is_____.

INDEPENDENT PRACTICE

Language Arts

Use all statements to draw conclusions such as the following:
- All easy books have pictures. "Pat the Bunny" is an easy book. So we know_____.
- All vowels are letters in the alphabet. "A" is a vowel. So we know _____.

Math

- All numbers that end in 4 are even numbers. 74 ends in 4. So we know_____.
- All rectangles have 4 sides. A square is a rectangle. So we know _____.

Science

- All mammals bear live young. A whale is a mammal. So we know _____.
- All reptiles are cold blooded. A snake is a reptile. So we know _____.

CATEGORICAL SYLLOGISM (continued)

Social Studies	• All states in the United States have a capital. Michigan is a state so we know_____.
	• All people who are born in the United States are citizens of the United States. Bob was born in Detroit, Michigan. So we know that_____.

Use the above examples to discuss reversals. All Statements cannot be reversed.

All things that fly are not airplanes.
All students are not third graders.
All insects are not butterflies.
All letters of the alphabet are not vowels.

PROVIDING INFORMATION—NO STATEMENTS

Student Rules:	• No Statements begin with the word "no" instead of all. The statement may also imply "no." No Statements can be reversed and still be true.
Model Skill:	Use the following statements as examples:
	• No frogs can talk. Therefore, nothing that talks is a frog.
	• No books have wheels. Therefore, nothing with wheels is a book.
	• No insects have fur. Therefore, nothing with fur is an insect.
	• Cats can't fly. Therefore, nothing that flies is a cat.
Guided Practice:	Use the following examples:
	• No animals are purple. Therefore, nothing that is purple is an animal.
	• No cars can walk. Therefore, nothing _____.
	• No fish can have legs. Therefore, _____.

INDEPENDENT PRACTICE

Language Arts	Use No Statements to illustrate rules such as the following:
	• No declarative sentences end with a question mark. Therefore, no sentences that end with a ? are declarative.
Math	• No subtraction problems have an addition sign. Therefore, _____.
Science	Use No Statements in concept development.
	• No birds have four legs. Therefore, _____.
	• No herbivores eat meat. Therefore_____.
Social Studies	• No democratic society has a king (monarch). Therefore, _____.
	• No tropical areas receive snowfall. Therefore, no area with snowfall is tropical.

MATRIX LOGIC

DEFINITION
Matrix logic problems organize information in order to solve problems through the use of a matrix table.

OBJECTIVE AND PURPOSE
Students learn how to gather information from clues and to record this information.

PROVIDING INFORMATION

Guidelines:

1. First read all clues and organize names and categories on the matrix.
2. Find all clues that give a definite yes or no. Mark "yes" with X's, "no" with O's. Remember when you mark a box with yes, you can fill in O's both horizontally and vertically.
3. Find clues that do not give complete information and try to relate it to other clues.
4. Find two or more clues that fit together to give enough information to mark boxes "Yes" or "No."

Model Skill:

Use the following problem to introduce students to matrix logic problems:

- Bob, Bruce, and Bill are related to Betty, Barbara, and Bonnie. To find out which of these boys and girls are brothers and sisters, use the following clues:

	Bob	Bruce	Bill
Betty	1	2	3
Barbara	4	5	6
Bonnie	7	8	9

Clues:
1. Bruce and Barbara are twins.
2. All the children's names begin with B.
3. Bonnie does not know Bob.

Questions:
1. Which clue names a brother and sister? *1*
   In which square can you put an X for yes? *5*
2. Which clue names the children who are not related? *3*
   In which square can you put an O for no? *7*
3. Which clue does not help you decide who are brothers and sister? *2*
   Can you mark any squares on the grid? *No*
4. Who is Bob's sister? *Betty*
5. Who is Bonnie's brother? *Bill*

MATRIX LOGIC (continued)

Guided Practice: The following problems can be used to practice matrix logic. Use the following clues to find out which color balloon each child had.

	Red	Green	Blue	Orange
Betty				
George				
Robert				
Owen				

1. The color of each child's balloon is different from the first letter of his name.

2. Betty does not have a green balloon.

3. Owen chose a red balloon.

Answers: Betty had the orange balloon
George had the blue balloon
Robert had the green balloon
Owen had the red balloon

Use the following clues to determine the cost of the toys.

	$5.25	$1.75	$4.50
skates			
ball			
game			

1. The game cost less than the skates, but more than the ball.

2. The skates could not be purchased at the same store as the ball and the game.

3. The ball was the least expensive.

Answers: The skates cost $5.25
The ball cost $1.75
The game cost $4.50

MATRIX LOGIC (continued)

Sally, Bob, Charles, and Alice had chores to do.
Sally set the table.
Bob cleaned the garage.
Charles vacuumed the living room.
Alice dusted the furniture.

One the following day the children switched chores. Use the following clues to find out which chores the children did the next day

	Sally	Bob	Charles	Alice
set table				
clean garage				
vacuum				
dust				

1. Sally did the chore no one else wanted to do.
2. Charles was afraid he would break some dishes, but he did it anyway.
3. Bob did not do the same job.
4. Alice did her chore in the same room where she worked before.

Answers: Charles set the table
Sally cleaned the garage
Alice vacuumed
Bob dusted the furniture

INDEPENDENT PRACTICE

Language Arts

- Students can write their own logic problems.
- Logic problems can be used to increase vocabulary and reading comprehension. For example: Choose three types of literature and choose three names. Place categories and names on a matrix. Write clues which will determine what genre of literature each student prefers.

Math

- Logic problems can be used to teach concepts such as taller, shorter, value of money, ordering of numbers. For example: Choose four different ages and names of four children. Place ages and names on a matrix form. Write clues to solve a problem about ages.

MATRIX LOGIC (continued)

Science
- Logic problems can be used to reinforce the concepts learned in classification. For example: Make up a problem using three kinds of animal homes. Choose names of three animals. Place names and categories on a matrix. Select and fill in answers to the matrix. Write clues which will lead to the solution of your problem.

Social Studies
- Logic problems can be used to solve problems about occupations, recreation, presidents, etc. For example: Make up a problem using four kinds of occupations. Choose names of four individuals. Place names and occupations on a matrix. Write clues which will lead to the match of each person with the correct occupation.

ANALOGIES

DEFINITION

An analogy is a conparison between two things, and the comparison is used to determine the relationship between different sets of things.

OBJECTIVE AND PURPOSE

By solving analogies students learn to analyze the relationship between two things and determine a similar relationship between two new things. Analogies help build vocabulary skills and exercise flexible thinking.

PROVIDING INFORMATION

There are many types of analogies such as the following:
* Synonym to antonym: yell is to whisper
* Part is to whole or whole is to part: core is to apple
* Function to thing: cook is to stove
* Characteristic is to thing: smooth is to glass
* Product is to thing or thing to product: milk is to cow

Guidelines:

1. Decide upon the relationship between the first two words.
2. State the relationship: Car is to tire because_____.
3. Examine the third word.
4. Select a fourth word which will make the third-fourth word have the same relationship as the first-second.
5. Be ready to explain your fourth word selection.

Model Skill:

Use the steps listed above with examples such as below:
* On is to off as start is to _____.
  (stop, opposites)
* Nail is to finger as hair is to _____.
  (head, part to whole)
* Eye is to see as ear is to _____.
  (hear, thing is to function)
* Swift is to deer as slow is to _____.
  (turtle, characteristic is to thing)
* Wool is to sheep as egg is to _____.
  (chicken, product is to thing)

Be sure to think orally so students can see how you arrived at your fourth word selection.

Guided Practice:

Use examples such as the following:
* Good is to bad as night is to day.
* A ship is to sea as plane is to air.
* Writer is to a book as an illustrator is to a picture.
* Cut is to scissors as slice is to knife.
* Apple is to fruit as corn is to vegetable.
* Cup is to drink as plate is to eat.
* Gold is to mine as oil is to well.

ANALOGIES (continued)

- Few is to many as some is to all.
- Toe is to foot as finger is to hand.
- Fire is to hot as candy is to sweet.

INDEPENDENT PRACTICE

Language Arts
- Snow White is to fairy tale as _____ is to _____

Math
- 15 is to 150 as _____ is to _____.
- Ounce is to pound as _____ is to ____.

Science
- Lava is to volcano as _____ is to_____.
- Lizard is to reptile as _____ is to ____.

Social Studies
- George Washington is to Revolutionary War as _____ is to _____.
- Florida is to Ponce de Leon as _____ is to _____.

SYLLOGISMS

DEFINITION

A syllogism is a deductive scheme of formal argument consisting of three statements. The first two statements are called the premises. The third statement is the conclusion. If the conclusion can be supported by the two premises, it is valid. If the conclusion cannot be supported by the two premises, it is invalid.

OBJECTIVE AND PURPOSE

Syllogisms are taught to students to develop skill in deductive reasoning.

PROVIDING INFORMATION

Guidelines:

1. The first statement is called premise 1.
2. The second statement is called premise 2.
3. Examine the first two statements to determine if the third statement or conclusion is valid (true) or invalid (false).

Model Skill:

Use the following examples to explain reasoning used to determine valid and invalid conclusions.

Example 1:

- All members of the cat family have four legs.
  A tiger is a cat.
  Therefore, a tiger has four legs.

  This is a valid conclusion. If a tiger is a cat and all cats have four legs, then a tiger must have four legs.

Example 2:

- All beets are vegetables.
  All beets are red.
  Therefore, all vegetables are red.

  This is an invalid conclusion. There is not proof that all vegetables are red. Remember, you cannot reverse an all statement. "All beets are red" cannot be reversed to mean all vegetables are beets.

Example 3:

- All horses eat hay.
  An Arabian is a horse.
  Therefore, Arabians eat hay.

  This is a valid conclusion. If an Arabian is a horse, and all horses eat hay, then an Arabian must eat hay.

SYLLOGISMS (continued)

Guided Practice:

1. All trout are fish.
   All fish swim.
   Therefore, trout can swim. (valid)

2. All squares have four sides.
   No four sided figures are triangles.
   Therefore, no squares are triangles. (valid)

3. All frogs croak.
   All frogs are amphibians.
   Therefore, all amphibians croak. (invalid)

4. All teachers are hard workers.
   Mrs. Smith is a teacher.
   Therefore, Mrs. Smith is a hard worker. (valid)

5. Algae is a plant.
   Algae grows in water.
   Therefore, all plants grow in water. (invalid)

6. Dairy products are good for you.
   Milk is a dairy product.
   Therefore, milk is good for you. (valid)

INDEPENDENT PRACTICE

Students can use the deductive reasoning of syllogisms to evaluate understanding of concepts in all subject areas.

Language Arts
- Given two premises, students can write a conclusion.
  I do not like anything that tastes sour.
  A lemon is sour. Therefore, _____.

Math
- Use syllogisms with concepts of shapes.
  Use syllogisms for deductive reasoning in problems such as the following:
  All X are Y.
  All X are Z.
  Therefore, _____. (all Z are Y)

Science
- Use syllogisms with scientific concepts.
  Insects have three body parts. A moth is an insect.
  Therefore, _____.

Social Studies
- Use deductive reasoning with social studies concepts.
  All presidents of the United States are elected by a vote of the people. Harry Truman was president.
  Therefore,_____.

BLOOM'S TAXONOMY

DEFINITION

Bloom's Taxonomy is a classification of thinking organized by level of complexity. Knowledge, Comprehension, Application, Analysis, Synthesis, and Evaluation are the six levels with Knowledge being the easiest or lowest level of thinking.

OBJECTIVE AND PURPOSE

Through direct instruction of each level of the taxonomy, students will understand the hierarchy of the thinking levels. They will see how each is dependent of and related to the preceding levels. Understanding the terminology of Bloom's Taxonomy will enable students to evaluate the type of thinking task that is required.

PROVIDING INFORMATION

Guidelines:

The following pages provide the teacher with a list of verbs and products which can be used at each level. A description of each level is provided. Lessons can be taught through content or through the use of *Gerfuls* by Cheryl Myers, Thinking Caps, Inc., Phoenix, Arizona.

KNOWLEDGE

DEFINITION

Knowledge is the ability to recognize, memorize, or recall information. It is the easiest level of thinking.

OBJECTIVE AND PURPOSE

Knowledge is the foundation which supports the higher levels of thinking.

PROVIDING INFORMATION

Guidelines:

1. Pay attention in class.
2. Listen and absorb information.
3. Remember.
4. Practice and drill.
5. Covers information in book.
6. Recognize information that has been covered.

Model Skill:

Read the following paragraph and answer the knowledge questions that follow.

The manatee or "sea cow" is a large mammal that lives in warm shallow salt water. One species of manatee lives in the rivers, bays, and lagoons along the coast of Florida.

The manatee is a gentle sea creature which grows to about fifteen feet in length and weighs about fifteen hundred pounds. It uses its front flippers to push seaweed and other water plants to its mouth. The mother usually has a single calf which she nurses.

The manatee is becoming scarce because of the destruction of their habitat. Many manatees are being injured by boat propellers. Scientists are studying the manatee in order to learn more about the species.

1. What is another name for the manatee?
2. Where does the manatee live?
3. What does a manatee eat?
4. Who is studying the manatee?

Guided Practice:

Use content material to have students answer knowledge questions.

Following are verbs that are used at the knowledge level:

Repeat	Recall
Label	Remember
Name	Describe
Quote	List

KNOWLEDGE (continued)

INDEPENDENT PRACTICE

The following products are used at the knowledge level:

> Chart
> Model
> Worksheet
> Labeled diagram
> Hand-drawn map

Language Arts
- Answer a worksheet based on a story you have read.
- Memorize and repeat a poem.

Math
- Describe the characteristics of a square.
- Remember the multiplication facts.

Science
- Label the parts of an insect.
- Name the characteristics of a mammal.

Social Studies
- Draw a map of Michigan and locate five important cities.
- Quote one of the amendments to the Constitution.

COMPREHENSION

DEFINITION

Comprehension is the lowest level of simple understanding. Students begins to attach meaning to facts and information.

OBJECTIVE AND PURPOSE

Comprehension requires the student to make use of the knowledge he or she has gained.

PROVIDING INFORMATION

Guidelines:

1. Can intelligently discuss and explain information.
2. Translates information into own words.
3. Interprets information from technical terms to familiar terms.

Model Skill:

Using the information on manatees:
1. Describe a manatee in your own words.
2. Discuss the reason that scientists are studying manatees.

Guided Practice:

Use content material to have students show that they understand the material.

Some verbs used at the comprehension level are

Restate	Discuss
Describe	Explain
Identify	Review
Summarize	Locate

INDEPENDENT PRACTICE

The following products are used at the comprehension level:
Teaching a lesson
Report
Timeline
Diorama

Language Arts

- Retell the story of _____ in your own words.
- Summarize the traits of a character in a story.

Math

- Tell in your own words the steps involved in solving a story problem.
- Explain how to do a subtraction problem which involves regrouping.

Science

- Discuss how matter is classified.
- Restate the definition of symmetry and describe where it is found in nature.

Social Studies

- Locate the Great Lakes on a map.
- Describe the first Thanksgiving.

APPLICATION

DEFINITION	Application is the ability to use or apply knowledge in a new situation.
OBJECTIVE AND PURPOSE	At the application level of Bloom's Taxonomy students will demonstrate the ability to use knowledge in a practical or problem solving situation.

PROVIDING INFORMATION

Guidelines:
1. Demonstrate use of knowledge.
2. Construct projects, models, or experiments.
3. Solve novel problems.

Model Skill:

Use the story of the manatee to demonstrate questions you might use to interview the scientist who is studying the manatee. For example:
1. How do you count the number of manatee?
2. How can you identify a manatee to keep track of its migration?
3. What is being done to save the manatee?

Guided Practice:

Use content material to have students demonstrate the application of knowledge. The following verbs are used at the application level:

Demonstrate	Use	Dramatize
Show	Construct	Apply
Illustrate	Operate	

INDEPENDENT PRACTICE

The following products are used at the application level:

Experiment	Story
Model	Role playing

Language Arts
- Write a diary for a character in a story.
- Sketch a picture to show the feelings of the main character toward the villain.

Math
- Put information into graph form.
- How would you use the principle of estimation outside school?

Science
- Demonstrate the correct use of a piece of equipment such as a balance.
- Conduct an experiment to demonstrate an electrical circuit.

Social Studies
- Plan plays, posters, contests, etc. to promote school spirit.
- Construct a model of a neighborhood.

ANALYSIS

DEFINITION	Analysis is the skill of taking apart information to identify the component parts and understand relationships.
OBJECTIVE AND PURPOSE	Through analysis of elements the student is able to understand the organizational structure. Analysis of material enables the student to see the relationships between ideas.

PROVIDING INFORMATION

Guidelines:
1. Identify ways to break the problem into parts.
2. Define each part clearly.
3. Identify and organize data related to each part.
4. State conclusion based on analysis.

Model Skill:
Using the knowledge of the manatee, compare and contrast a manatee and a whale. Analyze the reasons for manatees becoming an endangered species.

Guided Practice:
Use content material and have students analyze the information. The following verbs are used at this level:

Compare	Categorize
Contrast	Debate
Diagram	Relate
Examine	Order

INDEPENDENT PRACTICE

The following products are useful in analysis activities:

Diagram	Outline
Survey	Graph
Questionnaire	Debate
Chart	Family Tree

Language Arts
- Analyze the problems of familiar nursery rhymes.
- Compare and contrast two stories about animals. How are they alike? How are they different?

Math
- Differentiate between multiplication and addition.
- Outline steps involved in division.

Science
- Diagram the food chain of an owl.
- Differentiate between homemade soup with the kind you buy in a store.

Social Studies
- Graph the results of a survey questionnaire.
- Compare the Christmas holiday season with another holiday.

SYNTHESIS

DEFINITION

Synthesis means to put together elements or parts into a new whole, to create an orginal product.

OBJECTIVE AND PURPOSE

Synthesis is a divergent thinking skill in which students are encouraged to discover and explore new ways of doing things. It allows students to create, invent, and discover.

PROVIDING INFORMATION

Guidelines:

1. Identify the purpose for the product.
2. List basic elements which will be included in the product.
3. Organize ideas.
4. Develop a plan and create the new product.

Model Skill:

Using the information about the manatee, develop an original plan to prevent the manatee from being hurt by boat propellers. For example: Create an area designed for manatees in which boats are prohibited.

Guided Practice:

Use content area and have students create something new. Following are some erbs used at the synthesis level:

Create	Imagine (What If?)
Invent	Improve
Compose	Produce
Devise	

INDEPENDENT PRACTICE

The following products are examples of synthesis:

Story	Mural
Poem	Dance
Invention	Puppet Show
Play	Poster

Language Arts

- Rewrite the ending for a story.
- Find an unusual way to present a book report.

Math

- Design a poster to show the uses of math.
- Propose an unusual way to save money.

Science

- Invent a machine that will ...
- What if there were no insects?

Social Studies

- Revise the way to organize our schools.
- Write newspaper articles about a theme such as "Life in a Big City."

EVALUATION

DEFINITION

Evaluation is the sixth highest level of thinking in Bloom's Taxonomy. To evaluate is to judge or appraise the worth, value, or quality of an idea, an object, or an activity.

OBJECTIVE AND PURPOSE

Students will learn how to judge quality based on sound criteria and to effectively support or reject ideas. They will be able to make a firm commitment which they can defend and support.

PROVIDING INFORMATION

Guidelines:

1. Identify what is to be evaluated.
2. Establish criteria for evaluation.
3. Collect data related to each criteria.
4. Evaluate based on criteria.
5. Make final determination.

Model Skill:

Using information on manatees, decide which plan developed would best protect the manatee. Criteria could include cost, time, public acceptance, and how difficult the plan would be to implement.

Guided Practice:

Use content material to have students evaluate a product or an idea. Following are verbs used at this level:

Rank	Decide	Conclude
Choose	Support	Grade
Evaluate	Prioritize	

INDEPENDENT PRACTICE

The following products can be used at the evaluation level:

Editiorial	Self-evaluation
Court Trial	Panel Evaluation
Recommendation	Statement or Conclusion

Language Arts

- Decide which of two stories is the most logical portrayal of an incident.
- Determine if your essay meets established criteria.

Math

- Rank a variety of plans to help low achieving students with math as to which would be the most effective.
- Evaluate your solution to a story problem.

Science

- Evaluate results of an experiment.
- Determine criteria necessary for good resource.

Social Studies

- Have a debate on the Revolutionary War. Present both sides of the issue.
- Have court trial based on a current event or on a story such as "Jack and the Beanstalk."

PLANNING

DEFINITION

Planning is a method to develop a step-by-step procedure that will result in the achievement of a specific goal or outcome.

OBJECTIVE AND PURPOSE

Using the planning process will help students recognize the importance of organizing and planning in order to complete a task. Planning saves time and increases efficiency.

PROVIDING INFORMATION

Guidelines:

1. Identify the project and provide enough details to explain what is to be accomplished.
2. List the necessary materials to carry out the task.
3. List steps necessary to complete the task. Which job comes first, second, etc.? How much time is required?
4. Identify problems or difficulties that might occur.

Model Skill:

Use topics such as
- Planning a cheese sandwich.
- Planning a party.
- Giving a pet a bath.

The following format can be used to record responses:

WHAT	MATERIALS
1. Party	1. Invitations 2. Prizes 3. Decorations 4. Games 5. Food

STEPS	PROBLEMS
1. Decide time and place 2. Get permission 3. List of people to invite 4. Write invitations 5. Mail invitations 6. Plan games 7. Plan food	1. Permission not given 2. No place to have party 3. Conflict with another party 4. Forget to mail invitations

Guided Practice:

- Make a plan to study your spelling words.
- Plan a mural about a topic such as drug abuse, playground safety.
- Plan a courtroom trial for a fairy tale such as "Hansel and Gretel" or "Jack and the Beanstalk."

PLANNING (continued)

INDEPENDENT PRACTICE

Language Arts
- Plan a speech.
- Plan a vocabulary booklet.

Math
- Plan a lesson on measurement. Use cups, pints, quarts.
- Plan ways to memorize math facts.

Science
- Plan a demonstration or experiment.
- Plan a science fair project.

Social Studies
- Pretend that you are Christopher Columbus and plan the voyage.
- Plan a current event lesson for your class.

HYPOTHESIZING

DEFINITION

A hypothesis is a tentative statement about something that might or might not be true.

OBJECTIVE AND PURPOSE

A hypothesis statement is an important component of the scientific method. Students will learn the steps involved in research and methods used to prove or disprove a hypothesis.

PROVIDING INFORMATION

Guidelines:

1. Ask a question. State a preliminary hypothesis.
2. Gather information about the question - state reasons for hypothesis.
3. Refine statement so that it can be tested.
4. Test the hypothesis. Identify essential conditions and procedures for testing.
5. Analyze test data to see if the hypothesis is supported.

Model Skill:

Use statements such as the following:
1. Most children like ice cream better than candy.
2. Most fourth grade girls are taller than fourth grade boys.
3. Most students like to play baseball better than football.

Guided Practice:

Choose a question and pose a hypothesis that can be easily tested during the lesson. For example:
1. What color is the favorite of the girls in our class? Pink is the favorite color of girls in our class.
2. What would students prefer to be called? Students would rather be called kids than children.

INDEPENDENT PRACTICE

Language Arts

- The favorite type of book of students in my class is _____.
- Good characters in fairy tales are attractive while evil characters are ugly.

Math

- A page of single digit multiplication can be done faster with a calculator than without.
- The average allowance in our class is _____.

Science

- The higher the temperature, the faster the melting time of the ice.
- The more coils an electromagnet has, the greater its strength.

Social Studies

- The favorite lunch on this week's menu will be _____.
- George Washington did more for our country than Abraham Lincoln.

CoRT - PMI

DEFINITION	PMI is a way of treating ideas, suggestions, and proposals. P = Plus—The good things about an idea. M = Minus—The bad things about an idea. I = Interesting—The interesting things about an idea.
OBJECTIVE AND PURPOSE	Enhanced perception of an idea leads to more careful analysis. PMI encourages students to defer judgment and to explore all aspects of a situation before reaching a conclusion or decision.

PROVIDING INFORMATION

Guidelines:

1. List all the Plus (positive) aspects of the situation.
2. List all the Minus (negative) aspects of the situation.
3. List the Interesting aspects of the situation.
4. Examine all points before making decisions.

Model Skills:

Idea: All students must wear uniforms to school.

P: Students would not be teased about their clothes. Parents would not spend as much money on clothes for students.
M: Clothing stores would lose business. All students would look the same. Kids get tired of outfits.
I: There may not be as many clothing fads.

Guided Practice:

Use such ideas as the following:
1. Students should attend school during the summer.
2. Students may watch TV only one hour each day.

INDEPENDENT PRACTICE

Use PMI to discuss the following:

Language Arts
- Books reports are required by all students.
- A situation that occurs in a story (for example, having a monster for a friend).

Math
- Effects of a request for budget increases for school.
- Learning math facts is not necessary.

Science
- People should not be allowed to smoke in public.
- Windows should be made of plastic instead of glass.

Social Studies
- Pupils should have a say in making school rules.
- Students should be paid a small wage for attending school.

CoRT - CAF

DEFINITION	CAF is to Consider All Factors when making a decision or a plan.
OBJECTIVE AND PURPOSE	Doing a CAF will help students analyze their own thinking, as well as the thinking of others. A CAF can lead to more detailed critical thinking. Evaluation of all factors can help students determine both short term and long term consequences.

PROVIDING INFORMATION

Guidelines:

1. Do a CAF before choosing, deciding, or planning.
2. Consider all factors first, then decide on the most important factors.
3. Other people may be able to recognize factors you did not include.
4. If an important factor has been left out, the original decision may seem right, but later turn out wrong.
5. If you do a CAF on another person's thinking you may be able to tell what has been left out.

Model Skill:

Do a CAF on the question, "Shall I do my homework or not?"
1.0 What are the consequences of not turning it in?
    1.1   Will it lower my grade?
    1.2   Will the teacher be angry?
    1.3   Will I miss recess?
2.0 Do I need to do the homework?
    2.1   Do I understand the assignment?
    2.2   Do I need the practice?
    2.3   Do I need help?
3.0 Why can't I do it?
    3.1   After school activity
    3.2   TV program
    3.3   Forgot my book

Guided Practice:

Do a CAF on such decisions as the following:
1. Buying a new pair of jeans.
2. Extending the school year.
3. Lowering age at which students can drop out of school.

INDEPENDENT PRACTICE

Language Arts
- Do a CAF in choosing a book to read.

Math
- Do a CAF on the cost of food at a restaurant.
- Do a CAF on taking advance math courses.

Science
- Do a CAF on a new invention such as Star Wars.
- Do a CAF in setting up an experiment.

Social Studies
- Do a CAF on choosing a career.
- Do a CAF on raising taxes.

INFERENCES

DEFINITION

Inference is the skill of drawing a possible conclusion, consequence, or implication from a set of facts or premises.

OBJECTIVE AND PURPOSE

Inferences are used to help determine what might logically follow even though specific data is not stated. Prediction is an important step in the problem solving process.

PROVIDING INFORMATION

Guidelines:

1. Examine all the information given.
2. Identify the relevant information.
3. Decide what is missing. What would you like to know?
4. Use the given information to make a logical conclusion about the missing information.

Model Skill:

Use examples such as the following:

Sue put sandwiches, sunglasses, and suntan lotion in her bag. After a long drive Sue's mother visited friends while Sue enjoyed water, salty spray, and sun.

Every Wednesday, the school cafeteria serves pizza. Today is Wednesday.

Students and teachers left the building together before 3:00 p.m. and stood quietly outside.

The following questions are important in making an inference:
1. What do you think someone will do?
2. What do you think was meant by?
3. Why do you suppose?
4. What evidence will support the inference?

Guided Practice:

Can you explain why?

1. Wendy has finished giving her oral book report and she is smiling. The other students are clapping.
2. Tom's lunch is gone and his books are missing. Tom stopped to play on the way to school.
3. Sue stops to examine a scrape on her knee. She is wearing roller skates. A large dog is running down the street.
4. Friday morning was wet and cold, so Ned wore his raincoat and boots to school. Friday afternoon was sunny. Over the weekend it rained again. Ned got wet and cold delivering newspapers.
5. Sally baked bread in class. She tried to follow the recipe carefully and stopped several times to discuss what she was doing with friends. Sally was surprised when her bread turned out heavy and flat.

INFERENCES (continued)

INDEPENDENT PRACTICE

Language Arts
- Read a sampling of an author's prose and/or poetry and infer what the autho's life might have been like (time period, country, social and marital status, personal philosophy, and so on).
- Infer meanings of sentences when read with different punctuation and expression.

Math
- John likes math and appears to understand the concepts and processes. Yet, John does not do well on tests. Why?
- Study the player statistics of an All-Star baseball game, and infer who the most valuable player is.

Science
- Find out how animal tracking is done and note how inference is used. Using this thinking skill, do some of your own field work.
- Describe a type of machine or tool and have students infer its uses.

Social Studies
- Listen to a courtroom trial and explain why the verdict was issued.
- Read about the climate of any state and infer what its principle crops might be.

FORECASTING

DEFINITION	Forecasting involves predicting outcomes based on consideration of possible causes and/or effects of a given situation.
OBJECTIVE AND PURPOSE	Forecasting will expand students' ability to recognize cause and effect. Forecasting will encourage students to pre-plan, calculate, and use forethought or foresight. Predictions are based on inferences.

PROVIDING INFORMATION

Guidelines:
1. Consider all of the possible causes and effects of a given situation.
2. Examine the quality of each prediction.
3. Choose the best cause and/or effect.
4. Give several reasons for the choice.

Model Skill:
Examine "what if" statements such as
- What if candy bars cost $1.00?
- What if it rained pennies?
- What if people had horses instead of automobiles?

Guided Practice:
- Forecast the effects of not doing your homework.
- What would be the cause and effects of having no water at school?
- What if people had two heads?
- Give the causes/effects of gas stations being closed.

INDEPENDENT PRACTICE

Language Arts
- Stop at appropriate intervals while reading a story and predict what will happen next. Give reasons for your prediction.
- Write a sequel to a story you have read.

Math
- What would happen if the United States changed to the metric system tomorrow?
- Discuss the effects of using calculators in math class.

Science
- Predict the weather for a certain period of time.
- Consider the causes and effects of the continued destruction of forests.

Social Studies
- What if England had won the Revolutionary War?
- Discuss the causes and effects of unemployment in your state.

DECISION MAKING

DEFINITION

Decision making is the ability to decide or form a fixed intention. Through a systematic process, alternatives are examined in order to select one to solve a problem or reach a goal.

OBJECTIVE AND PURPOSE

Through teaching the decision-making process, students learn how to make choices based on examination of alternatives in terms of defined criteria. Decision making is a skill students will use throughout life.

PROVIDING INFORMATION

Guidelines:

1. State the problem or goals.
2. List alternatives to the situation.
3. Establish criteria by which to examine the alternatives.
4. Rank alternatives according to criteria.
5. Choose the best alternative.
6. Evaluate choice: Defend your decision by giving several reasons for your choice.

Model Skill:

Use ideas such as the following:

Step 1   Decide what gift you want for your birthday.

Step 2   List alternatives.

Step 3   Criteria: Do I need it?

Can my friend afford it?

Is it readily available?

INDUCTIVE REASONING

DEFINITION

Inductive reasoning entails reasoning from the specific to the general to produce a concept.

OBJECTIVE AND PURPOSE

Given familiar concepts or concrete items with common characteristics, students will be able to produce their own concept.

PROVIDING INFORMATION

Guidelines:

From specific to concept:
1. Collect organize and label data.
2. Identify common characteristics or what is generally true.
3. State a generalization based on common characteristics.
4. Check against data to see if generalization holds up.

Model Skill:

Use such examples as the following:
1. What do the following people have in common? *Abraham Lincoln, Theordore Roosevelt, Thomas Jefferson, George Washington* Answer: They were all Presidents of the United States.

2. What is similar about the following objects? *kite, bird, helicopter, airplane* Answer: They are things that fly.

Guided Practice:

The following questions and instructions require students to reason inductively to produce a concept.

The main idea is _____. What do _____ have in common? Summarize _____. What do _____ represent?

What do the following represent: *Chicago, Dallas, Philadelphia, Detroit* Answer: They are U.S. cities.

What are the following? *Dachshunds, Poodles, German Shepards* Answer: They are types of dogs.

Give examples of fairy tales and ask what they are.

INDEPENDENT PRACTICE

Language Arts
- Give examples of parts of speech and ask what they are.
- Have students read a short story and give the story a title.

Math
- Give examples of triangles and ask what they are.
- Have students identify several fractions as proper.

Science
- Give examples of liquids and ask what they are.
- Identify a list of birds as birds of prey.

Social Studies
- Have students identify a list of cities and state capitals.
- By noting such characteristics as plantation homes, slavery, fields of cotton and tobacco, students could reason inductively that the South was chiefly an agricultural area.

DEDUCTIVE REASONING

DEFINITION Deductive thinking requres the ability to provide one's own supporting examples, illustration, or application of a given concept. Deductive thinking moves from a generalization to supporting detail.

OBJECTIVE AND PURPOSE Given a familiar concept, students will be able to produce their own examples of the concept. Deductive thinking assists both oral and written communication as examples of a concept will lead to a better understanding.

PROVIDING INFORMATION

Guidelines:
1. Present the generalization and clarify the concept.
2. List the defining criteria of the generalization.
3. Determine examples of the concept by recalling examples that match the criteria.
4. Apply examples to generalization. Describe to show that they meet the criteria.

Model Skill:
- Give examples of things that occur during a season such as winter.
- Provide details that support the conclusion that winter is cold.

Guided Practice:
- Give examples of verbs.
- Name at least two kinds of luxury cars.
- Provide examples of mammals.
- Give examples of school safety rules.

INDEPENDENT PRACTICE

Language Arts
- Provide examples of fairy tales.
- Give examples of autobiographies.

Math
- Provide examples of odd numbers.
- List examples of where you might find percentages used.

Science
- Provide examples of carniverous animals.
- Provide examples of foods that contain starch.

Social Studies
- Name several European countries.
- Provide examples of constitutional amendments.

DILEMMAS

DEFINITION

A dilemma is a problem having two equally represented alternatives. Dilemmas may emerge from at least three sources: specific course content, current societal issues, situations related to lives of students. Ingredients in a dilemma story are 1) Focus (problem); 2) Central Character; 3) Choice—two alternative solutions which present a definite conflict for the character. What should the character do?

OBJECTIVE AND PURPOSE

Students faced with dilemmas should be able to analyze the alternatives, make choices, and learn to respect another point of view.

PROVIDING INFORMATION

Guidelines:

1.0 State the dilemma.
    1.1   Explain terminology as necessary.
    1.2   Make sure focus problem is defined.

2.0 State tentative position.
    2.1   Reflect on individual position.
    2.2   Establish position and state reasons.
    2.3   Share position.

3.0 Examine reasons.
    3.1   Examine reasons in small groups.
        3.1.1   Homogeneous decisions
        3.1.2   Heterogeneous decisions

    3.2   Examine different positions of all groups.
        3.2.1   Issues. What other issues are involved other than the main problem?
        3.2.2   Analogies. Think of similar situations and how they were resolved.
        3.2.3   Consequences. What will be the consquences of each position?

    3.3   Reflect on individual position.
        3.3.1   Summarize all reasoning.
        3.3.2   State final choice.
        3.3.3   Justify choice.

Model Skill:

- Use the steps in dilemma reasoning to do the following:

You have promised to babysit for your neighbor Saturday night. Your friend asks you to come to her sleep over that same night. What should you do?

DILEMMAS (continued)

Guided Practice: The following problems may be used:

After you get home from the store you realize the clerk has given you a $10 bill instead of a $1 bill. What should you do?

You are at a friend's house with a group of kids. They decide to sneak some cigarettes and smoke. What should you do?

Your best friend did not do his homework. He asks to copy your paper so that he won't get in trouble. If you refuse, he says he won't be your friend. What should you do?

Language Arts
- Write a dilemma of your own for other people to solve.
- Find the dilemma posed in a story. Predict the choice the character will make and discuss how this decision will affect the story.

Math
- Bob wants to go to camp. He needs to earn $100 to pay for his registration. He could get a job delivering papers after school, but the coach has asked him to try out for the basketball team. What should he do?
- A construction company is building a new home. As a foreman on the job, you find out they are using inferior materials to cut costs. What should you do?

Science
- Should America be spending money exploring outer space or using the money for social programs such as low income housing?
- Discuss the dilemma of people wanting larger, more comfortable cars and the need to conserve oil.

Social Studies
- A large manufacturing company is no longer making a profit. The president of the company tells the workers that either some of them will lose their jobs or everyone must take a pay cut. As union president, how would you advise the workers?
- Discuss the dilemma of a city council in the choice of dividing and selling productive farmland to use as additional homesites.

THINKING ERRORS

DEFINITION

Thinking errors may occur when

> Facts and opinions are confused.
> Emotion is used instead of evidence.
> The evidence is insufficient, or one example proves the rule.
> Real and fanciful concepts are confused.
> There is only one way to do it.

OBJECTIVE AND PURPOSE

By discussing common errors in thinking, students will be made aware of the elements of faulty reasoning. They will be encouraged to check elements in their thinking.

PROVIDING INFORMATION

Model Skills:

Use newspaper, television, or magazine ads that use persuasion or propaganda techniques that rely on faulty reasoning. Discuss thinking errors. For example,

Everyone is hurrying to our biggest sale! Buy now before it is too late! This great sale ends Saturday!

Guided Practice:

"I've tried dozens of other diets. Nothing worked until I tried this "X" plan. I have lost 150 pounds."

"I trust the experts. The experts recommend Brand X, so buy the brand used by the experts."

INDEPENDENT PRACTICE

Language Arts

- Students can write an ad that uses clear thinking.
- Discuss choice of words and exaggeration in writing, such as great, super, best ever, spectacular.

Math

- Discuss use of faulty statistics.

Science

- Discuss omission of facts. For example, what facts has the media left out in their discussion of nuclear power plant accidents so that people are unaware of the true extent of danger.

Social Studies

- Discuss quotes taken out of context.
- Discuss techniques such as testimonials or name calling used by politicians to encourage people to vote for them.

REFERENCES

Broomell, B. and Griffin, D. (1984). *What If?*. East Aurora, New York: D.O.K. Publishers.

Broomell, B. and Griffin, D. (1985). *What If? Primary*. East Aurora, NewYork: D.O.K. Publishers.

Clements, S., & Kolbe, and K. Villapando E. (1983). *Do-It-Yourself Critical and Creative Thinking*. Phoenix, Arizona: Kathy Kolbe Concept, Inc.

deBono, Edward (1975). *CoRT Thinking, CoRT*, teacher notes. Elmsford, New York: Pergamon Press.

Leimbach, J. (1986). *Primarily Logic*. San Luis Obispo, California: Dandy Lion Publications.

Myers, Cheryl (1982). *Gerfuls*. Phoenix, Arizona: Thinking Caps, Inc.

Polette, N. (1987). *The ABC's of Books and Thinking Skills*. O'Fallon, Missouri: Book Lures, Inc.

Post, B. and Cads (1982). Fearon Teacher Aids, a division of David S. Lake Publishers, Belmont, California.

Risby, B. (1983). *Thinking Through Analogies*. San Luis Obispo, California: Dandy Lion Publications.

Risby, B. (1987). *Logic Countdown*. San Luis Obispo, California: Dandy Lion Publications.

Risby, B. (1987). *Logic Liftoff*. San Luis Obispo, California: Dandy Lion Publications.

Schoenfield, M. and Rosenblatt J. (1985). *Adventures with Logic*. Belmont, California: David S. Lake Publishers.

Schoenfield, M. and Rosenblatt J. (1985). *Discovering Logic*. Belmont, California: David S. Lake Publishers.

Schoenfield, M. and Rosenblatt J. (1985). *Playing with Logic*. Belmont, California: David S. Lake Publishers.

Talents Unlimited. Mobile, Alabama: Mobile County Public Schools.

Wellner, B. & Yoder J. (1985). *Productive Thinking and Planning*. East Aurora, New York: D.O.K. Publishers.

BIBLIOGRAPHY

Bloom, E., Engelhart, M., Furst E., Hill W. H., Krathwohl, D. (1956). *Taxonomy of educational objectives, handbook I: cognitive domain.* New York: David McKay Co.

Beyer, B. (1988). *Developing a thinking skills program.* Boston, Massachusetts: Allyn and Bacon, Inc.

Beyer, B. (1987). *Practical strategies for the teaching of thinking.* Boston, Massachusetts: Allyn and Bacon, Inc.

Costa, A. (1985). *Developing minds.* Alexandria, Virginia: Association for Supervision and Curriculum Development.

Davis, G. (1983). *Creativity is forever.* Dubuque, Iowa: Kendall/Hunt Publishing Co.

Ennis, R. (1962). A critical concept of critical thinking. *Harvard Review,* Vol. 32, No. 1, Winter 1962.

Galbraith, R. and Jones, T. (1976). *Moral reasoning, a teaching handbook for adapting Kohlberg to the classroom.* Greenhaven Press, Inc.

Nickerson, R., Perkins, D., Smith L. (1985). *Teaching thinking.* Hillsdale, New Jersey: Laurence Erlbaum.

Renzulli, J., Reis, S. (1985). *Schoolwide enrichment model: a comprehensive plan for educational excellence.* Mansfield Center, Connecticut: Creative Learning Press, Inc.

Williams, F. (1970). *Classroom ideas for encouraging thinking and feeling.* Buffalo, New York: D.O.K. Publishers.

Appendix

THINKING SKILLS
SCOPE AND SEQUENCE
GRADES K–5

CREATIVE THINKING SKILLS

Kindergarten	*First Grade*	*Second Grade*
Fluency	Fluency	Flexibility
Curiosity	Originality	Modification
Imagery	Associative Thinking	Elaboration

Third Grade	*Fourth Grade*	*Fifth Grade*
Brainstorming	Brainstorming	Forced Relationships
Modification	Creative Problem Solving	Synectics (Metaphors)
Creative Problem Solving	Attribute Listing	Creative Thinking Process

CRITICAL THINKING SKILLS

Kindergarten	*First Grade*	*Second Grade*
Classification	Classification	Webbing
Comparison	Cause and Effect	Logical Thinking (Introduction)
Patterning	Labeling	Planning
Sequence	Observation	Bloom's Taxonomy

Third Grade	*Fourth Grade*	*Fifth Grade*
Hypothesizing	Logic (Solving Analogies)	Logic
Bloom's Taxonomy	Forecasting	(Solving Analogies)
CoRT-PMI	Inferences	(Syllogisms)
	CoRT-CAF	Decision Making
		Inductive/Deductive Reasoning
		Dilemmas
		Thinking Errors